more Spice than Sugar

more Spice than Sugar

Poems About Feisty Females

Compiled by Lillian Morrison

Illustrated by Ann Boyajian

Houghton Mifflin Company
Boston 2001

The text of this book is set in 10.5-point Veljovic.

Library of Congress Cataloging-in-Publication Data

More spice than sugar: poems about feisty females /
compiled by Lillian Morrison; illustrated by Ann Boyajian.
p.   cm.
ISBN 0-618-06892-9
1. Women—Juvenile poetry. 2. Feminism—Juvenile
poetry. 3. Children's poetry, American. I. Morrison,
Lillian. II. Boyajian, Ann, ill.
PS595.W59 M67 2001
811'.5080352042—dc21
00-031947

Manufactured in the United States of America
RO 10 9 8 7 6 5 4 3 2 1

In memory of
Mura Dehn
and
M. C. Richards,
independent spirits and life-enhancers

— L.M.

Contents

Against the Odds

Notes

Preface

This collection of poems celebrating high-spirited girls and women has been a labor of love. When I was a youngster growing up in Jersey City, New Jersey, I roller-skated, played every kind of ball game in the streets, ran races around the block (there were no track teams for girls in my elementary or high school in those days), and dreamed of becoming a star athlete. I looked up to and identified with female sports figures, women aviators, explorers, and, eventually, as I matured, all adventurous, talented women in the arts, in science, in the struggle for human rights, in just plain living.

I have always loved poetry. I would have been delighted, when I was growing up, to find a whole book of poems about girls and women whose temperaments and achievements I could admire, especially if they went against the usual gender stereotypes (e.g., "Girls can't do that"). And so it was with much pleasure that I gathered these poems, most of them by contemporary poets, male and female. I hope they will delight, amuse, and, in some cases, inspire the present-day young reader.

the drum

daddy says the world is
a drum tight and hard
and i told him
i'm gonna beat
out my own rhythm

Nikki Giovanni

10

Yes, It Was My Grandmother

Yes, it was my grandmother
who trained wild horses for pleasure and pay.
People knew of her, saying:
    She knows how to handle them.
    Horses obey that woman.

She worked,
skirts flying, hair tied securely in the wind and dust.
She rode those animals hard and was thrown,
time and time again.
She worked until they were meek
and wanting to please.
    She came home at dusk,
    tired and dusty,
    smelling of sweat and horses.

She couldn't cook,
my father said smiling,
your grandmother hated to cook.

    Oh, Grandmother,
    who freed me from cooking.
    Grandmother, you must have made sure
    I met a man who would not share the kitchen.

    I am small like you and
    do not protect my careless hair
    from wind or rain—it tangles often,
    Grandma, and it is wild and untrained.

Luci Tapahonso

Pioneer Girl Driving West

Pull hard on the left rein,
shout, "Haw!" and their heads do go
where you want.
Pull hard on the right, shout "Gee!"
and watch out for ravines and gulleys.
Keep the wheels off the rocky shoulder
of the road,
if there is a road.
And if the oxen scare,
eyes rolling, horns tossing,
why, just hold on
and hope you don't die.

I'm not afraid. If I can cook
under an umbrella, wash clothes
in the swift rivers, and make sure
Nell don't fall under the wagon wheels,
I guess I can drive an old team of oxen.

Ann Turner

12

The Rebel

When I
die
I'm sure
I will have a
Big Funeral...
Curiosity
seekers...
coming to see
if I
am really
Dead...
or just
trying to make
Trouble...

Mari Evans

from Adventures of Isabel

Isabel met an enormous bear,
Isabel, Isabel, didn't care.
The bear was hungry, the bear was ravenous,
The bear's big mouth was cruel and cavernous.
The bear said, Isabel, glad to meet you,
How do, Isabel, now I'll eat you!
Isabel, Isabel, didn't worry;
Isabel didn't scream or scurry.
She washed her hands and she straightened her hair up,
Then Isabel quietly ate the bear up.

Ogden Nash

The Artist, Georgia O'Keeffe

georgia
was an outdoor girl
she loved the light
the air of any season
she climbed apple trees
rode atop hay wagons
sang when the wind
waved wildflowers
in fields as far
as the eye could see

georgia
was an outdoor girl
her comfortable ways
with earth & sky
never left her

Monica Kulling

[The Poet Emily]

They shut me up in Prose—
As when a little Girl
They put me in the Closet—
Because they liked me "still"—

Still! Could themself have peeped—
And seen my Brain—go round—
They might as wise have lodged a Bird
For Treason—in the Pound—

Emily Dickinson

Sylvia Earle: Deep Ocean Explorer

Her eyes might graze
    toward
        distant
            stars,
but not for her the lure of Mars.
She's challenged by a different place,
    just as unknown as outer space.
Not for her the stratosphere
    but a life-filled, liquid atmosphere—
where she can be...a pioneer!
        Down,
            down,
                down
                    in
        the depths of the sea
           where
                no human
had gone before.
        Down,
      down
        down
           to
the deepest deep—
      exploring
    the ocean floor.

Bobbi Katz

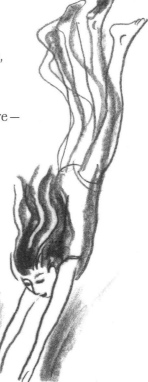

The Girl Who Makes the Cymbals Bang

I'm the girl who makes the cymbals bang—
It used to be a boy
That got to play them in the past
Which always would annoy

Me quite a bit. Though I complained,
Our teacher Mister Cash
Said, "Sorry, girls don't have the strength
To come up with a crash."

"Oh yeah?" said I. "Please give them here!"
And there and then, I slammed
Together those brass plates so hard
His eardrums traffic-jammed.

He gulped and gaped, and I could tell
His old ideas were bending—
So now me and my cymbals give
Each song a real smash ending.

X. J. Kennedy

Girl with Sampler
"A Soft Answer Turneth Away Wrath"

She sat by the window,
lips pursed, plying her needle.
The parlor wall waited
for a family showpiece.
"Do it right, child!" said her mother.
This way she learned the ABC's,
improved her mind with Bible verses,
embroidered her name into her dowry:
Nabby Dexter of Providence, Rhode Island,
Patricia Goodeshall, Abigail Fleetwood,
Elizabeth Finney, virtuoso of stitches
(cross . . . flat . . . buttonhole . . .
satin . . . outline . . . bullion knot).
Some prized the task and its performance,
others groaned as they ripped out blunders
in and around the moral sentences.
One of them added a line to her sampler:
"And Hated every bit of it."

Stanley Kunitz

If I Were a Kite

If I were a kite
I'd kneel,
stretch my skinny arms
out wide,
and wait for wind.

My yellow shirt would
fill up like a sail
and flap,
tugging my crisscrossed
wooden bones and me
toward seas of cloud.

My rippling paper skin
would rustle like applause
as I inhaled,
gulping one last gust
to swoop me giddy-quick
above the trees.

My red rag tail
would drift
toward everything green
to balance me

So all day
    I could
        loop and climb

      loop and climb

        and
        soar

into pure sky.

Jaqueline Sweeney

Conquering the Enemy

With this wide, unwieldy sword
    I stab the snow.
Jab-lift. Toss-drop.

Plunging into battle,
    I am Queen Boadicea
or some later lady-warrior.

A broad-bladed halberd
    in my hand,
I slice down to cement.

Though my enemy bleeds white
    and sends
a thousand reinforcements,

Still I carve a swath along
    this ambushed path.
Jab-lift. Toss-drop.

A woman warrior with wit and weapon,
    I can conquer what this world
thrusts down upon me.

Cynthia Pederson

When I Am Me

I'm impossible...possible,
breaking away from the
hard-holding hand
and flinging myself
in the air
on the sea
on a wave in the land
And thrashing about
just impossibly...possibly,
calling—no, yelling—
as loud as I can,
I am me!
I am me!
I can do anything.
I can run
to the end of the land
if I want to
or swim to the end of the sea
if I want to.
   I want to—not now,
   but I want to
   and will when it's possible...
   really is possible.
   Everything's possible
   when I am me.

Felice Holman

Family Eccentric

Marie is bald and doesn't
give a darn. To prove it
she often spits in public
and hates to wear a hat.

I hope she changes
for the better before
she learns to talk.

Edward Willey

Round the Bases

She hits the tee ball
like a soft breeze,
and picks wildflowers
on the way to first.

She hits the soft ball
like a young pro,
and skips along to claim
her rightful place on second.

She hits the hard ball
like a veteran,
running faster than most
and rests at third.

She hits the fast ball
like a woman on a mission,
amazing the boys
as she slides home.

Robert L. Harrison

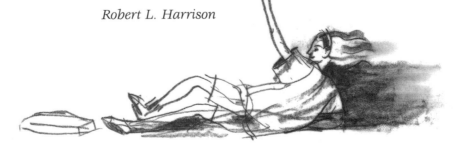

Rosie the Rollerblader

She puts on her helmet,
She fastens her pads.
No more skating on the old-time quads.
She's an in-line skater,
She's a rollerblader
Gliding all over the town.

She's an acrobat
On the toughest rails.
She's a leader on the hilly trails.
So take to your heels
When she's on wheels
Or her speed will mow you down.

Lillian Morrison

I Want to Swim

I want to swim.
Really swim.
Not just splash my arms
and legs and sink,
but swim.

I want to dive.
Really dive.
Not just smack the water
with my feet,
but dive.

headfirst
from poolside,

bubbles swirling
'round my body
as I glide.

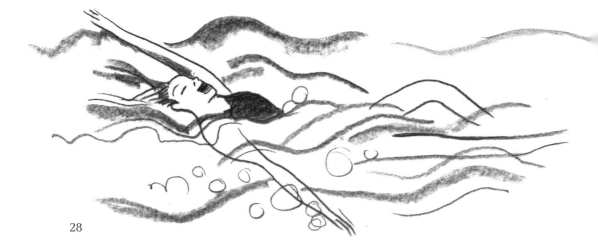

And topside
when I shake the hair
from my face,
pinch the water
from my eyes,

I'll finally see the others
far behind.

Let my feet be flippers,
arms be fins.

I want to swim.

Jacqueline Sweeney

Lashondra Scores!

She takes a

bl**o**ck! n**o**-look pass

off a from y**o**u and

c**o**ming banks it **o**ff the glass

Lash**o**ndra's f**o**r

cl**o**ck! tw**o**

on the

sec**o**nds left

only

J. Patrick Lewis

Lucky Sukey

Look out, here comes Lucky Sukey
Sucking on her mucky-looking cookie.

She can beat at baseball,
She can run like the wind,
She can chin the bar faster than it's
    ever been chinned.

Look out, here comes Lucky Sukey
Sucking on her mucky-looking cookie.
How can she always win? It's spooky!

X. J. Kennedy

Little League Southpaw

Her arm's a whirligig
winding up against the sky

She holds the game
in her left hand
and lets the ball F...L...Y!

   Strike one! Strike *two!* Strike THREE!

Letitia!
Our team's
brand-new
pitcher—
Full of herself,
The cream of this year's crop.

Patricia Hubbell

32

Fastest Woman in the World
for Florence Griffith Joyner

Florence, flashing her nails of red,
    glamorously groomed from foot to head;
Leaving poverty far behind,
    vigorously trained in body and mind.
Overcoming adversity,
    role for what a woman can be;
Jessie Owens Award on her shelf,
    set the highest goals for herself.
Olympic medals are hers to hold,
    winner of the silver and gold.

Anita Wintz

For Annie
on Her Unicycle

Looking down
on us all from
your perfect balance,
you are the stem
of the plum.

You wheel down the yard
easy as treading
water and take
the curb with a kind
of wit, as if you

didn't notice it
was there.
You are poised
as a peony. You
are a potted plant

that rose up
and pedaled the pot.
You are the Harlem
Globetrotters
trotting the globe.

When you turn
at the lilacs
to climb the drive,
how can anyone
ask you to

wash the dishes?

Conrad Hilberry

Aurelia Dobre: World Champion Gymnast

Spins clockwork,
then oscillates
between the bars.
Time waits
as she unwinds.
Walks the plank.
Defies natural order.
Points toes
to test the water.
Walks on that.
Skims and ducks
and drakes
across the mat.
Creates
ripples of applause.
Computes her vault
on magnetic
tape.
The kick
is muscle memory.
Traces her geometry;
spirals, circles.
No straight edge,
all curves, curls,
and smiles.

Chris Woods

Wilma Rudolph
(Who Won Three Golds in the 1960 Olympics)

She was the one who seemed
to run in the sky,
legs from nothing,
from nowhere,
her feet surrounded
by air.

Her smile went faster
than anyone else's.

La Gazelle Noire (the Black Gazelle).
The cinders were black;
she was the color of light;
three times more golden.

Her spikes ate the world.
Her knees bumped into clouds.
Her arms pushed the wind
out of the way.

No one could catch Wilma
who wore five magic rings:
red, yellow, green, white, black.

Grace Butcher

Joan Benoit

1984 U.S. Olympic Marathon Gold Medalist

During the third mile
not the eighteenth as expected
she surged ahead
leaving behind the press
of bodies, the breath
hot on her back
and set a pace
the experts claimed
she couldn't possibly keep
to the end.

Sure, determined,
moving to an inner rhythm
measuring herself against herself
alone in a field of fifty
she gained the twenty-six miles
of concrete, asphalt, and humid weather
and burst into the roar of the crowd
to run the lap around the stadium
at the same pace
once to finish the race
and then again in victory

and she was still fresh
and not even out of breath
and standing.

Rina Ferrarelli

The Hamill Camel
for Dorothy Hamill

stretched   out   like lightning

streaking   across   the sky

you spin spiraling,

fireworks on the 4th of July

until you

e x
p
l o d e

into

a

sit

spin.

Anita Wintz

First Lady of Sports
Mildred "Babe" Didrikson Zaharias
1914–1956

Let me tell you a little story
    About Babe Zaharias.
She walked like you and she talked like me,
    But she wasn't like any of us.

She was born in outback Texas
    Where the tall tall-tales grow,
And they stood in line to see her
    One-superwoman show.

Babe raced the wind and beat it,
    She high-hurdled the town,
She threw the javelin a mile—
    And caught it coming down.

Babe broad-jumped over Texas,
　　And put the shot so far
What landed in Oklahoma
　　Looked like a shooting star.

And then she took up golfing,
　　Had seventeen straight wins.
But that's not where the story ends,
　　It's where this tale begins.

"I'll win as many medals,"
　　She said when just a kid,
"As anyone who ever lived."
　　And that's just what she did.

J. Patrick Lewis

WNBA Stars

I holler and I whoop,
My heart goes loop-de-loop
When Houston Comets'
Swoopes and Cooper
Take it to the hoop.

Lillian Morrison

The Equestrienne

steps out of four-inch heels,
parades on the balls of her feet,

runs to leap and lands upright
arms outstretched on the black

broad black, then slides down
squeezing the barrel flanks

that ripple with a word, a touch:
a synchronized merging of muscle

and sweat, 4:30 in the afternoon
under a half-filled August tent.

Roger Pfingston

Most Valuable Player

If I had a trophy
I'd put it on the middle shelf
of my bookcase. I'd dust
it every day
and polish it once a week.

It would have a statue of a woman
holding a bat, her golden arm
cocked up a little
waiting for the pitch.
When my friends came over
I'd stand next to the bookcase casual-like
till they said, "Is that a trophy?"
I'd read the inscription every morning.
I'd ask someone to take my picture
with my trophy.

My trophy would say
"Softball Player" on the bottom,
and everyone would know
that in summer I tie on my cleats

run onto the field,
slapping high fives.
They'd know I take third base,
put my glove to the dry dirt,
scatter dust in the air.
They'd hear the fans shout,

"Hey, some catch!"
when that white ball comes slamming
into my glove,
and, "Watch out, she'll steal home,"
as my cleats dig and dig.
They'd feel the weight of the little statue
and think, "I bet she's going out
with her team tonight,"
"I bet she could teach me how to throw,"
"I bet she plays softball,"
and I do,

I do.

Sarah Van Arsdale

Behind the Mask

Who was that goalie
Who played the game?
Who stopped the pucks?
Who won us fame?

Who was that person
Who hung in there?
Who worked so hard?
Who did and dared?

Who was that goalie
Who saved the game?
Who brought us cheers?
Who knows her name?

Robert L. Harrison

Against
the
Odds

I May, I Might, I Must

If you can tell me why the fen
appears impossible, I then
will tell you why I think that I
can get across it if I try.

Marianne Moore

Women

They were women then
My mama's generation
Husky of voice — Stout of
Step
With fists as well as
Hands
How they battered down
Doors
And ironed
Starched white
Shirts
How they led
Armies
Headragged Generals
Across mined
Fields
Booby-trapped
Kitchens
To discover books
Desks
A place for us
How they knew what we
Must know
Without knowing a page
Of it
Themselves.

Alice Walker

Brave New Heights

I hear Amelia Earhart
took a plane
and flew it like a bullet
straight up through clouds
into an atmosphere
we can't see

and when the engine
cut
(the plane being pushed
as high as it would go)

I hear Amelia Earhart
turned that plane
straight back
down into a blanket
of foggy cloud lying thick
and nearly to the ground

only with the clouds gone
could she pull back on the stick
the ground screaming in her face
Amelia tacked that plane
back into the sky
saving herself and breaking
another flying record

Monica Kulling

Where Are You?

Anne Frank,
where are you?
Answer me, sing to me, talk to me.
In what blessed place
can I be near you?
In what place can I invoke your name
and cover the earth
with flowers?
Anne Frank,
though life for each of us
is not an everlasting flower,
we are all looking for you
as though you were still alive,
still sailing along, in your party dress,
putting into shore through
Amsterdam's canals
and your sparkling bicycle
were still waiting for you on the blue piers.

Marjorie Agosín
(translated from the Spanish
by Mónica Bruno)

Fannie Lou Hamer

fannie
lou
hamer
never
heard
of
in chicago
was known for
her
big
black
mouth
in the south
fannie lou
ate
her greens
watched
her land
and wanted
to
vote

men went
to the bottom
of the river
for wanting less
but fannie
got up
went to the courthouse

big as a fist
black as the ground
underfoot

Sam Cornish

The Many and the Few
For Rosa Parks, Part-time Seamstress,
Montgomery, Alabama, December 1, 1955

It was an Alabama day
For both the Many and the Few.
There wasn't really much to do;
No one had very much to say.

Until a bus, the 4:15,
Drove by. But no one chanced to see
It stop to pick up history.
The doors closed slowly on a scene:

The quiet seamstress paid her fare
And took the one seat she could find,
And, as it happened, just behind
The Many People sitting there.

The Many People paid no mind
Until the driver, J. P. Blake,
Told the Few of *them* to take
The deeper seats. But she declined.

Blake stopped the bus and called the police;
And Many a fire was set that night,
And Many a head turned ghostly white
Because she dared disturb the peace.

To celebrate the ride that marks
The debt the Many owe the Few,
That day of freedom grew into
The Century of Rosa Parks.

J. Patrick Lewis

from Elizabeth Blackwell

Now Elizabeth Blackwell, how about you?
Seamstress or teacher, which of the two?
You know there's not much else that a girl can do.
Don't mumble, Elizabeth. Learn to raise your head.

"I'm not very nimble with a needle and thread.
I could teach music—if I had to," she said.
"But I think I'd rather be a doctor instead."

"Is this some kind of joke?"
asked the proper menfolk.
"A woman be a doctor?
Not in our respectable day!
A doctor! An M.D.! Did you hear what she said?
She's clearly and indubitably out of her head!"

To medical schools she applied.
In vain.
And applied again
and again
and again
and one rejection offered this plan:
why not disguise herself as a man?
If she pulled back her hair, put on boots and pants,
she might attend medical lectures in France.
Although she wouldn't earn a degree,
they'd let her study anatomy.

Elizabeth refused to hide
her feminine pride.
She drew herself up tall
(all five feet one of her!)

and tried again.
And denied again.
The letters answering no
mounted like winter snow.

Until the day
when her ramrod will
finally had its way.
After the twenty-ninth try,
there came from Geneva, New York,
the reply
of a blessed
Yes!

Geneva,
Geneva,
how sweet the sound;
Geneva,
Geneva,
sweet sanctuary found...

...and the ladies of Geneva
passing by her in the street
drew back their hoopskirts
so they wouldn't have to meet.

The perfect happy ending
came to pass:
Elizabeth graduated...
...at the head of her class.

And the ladies of Geneva
all rushed forward now to greet
that clever, dear Elizabeth,
so talented, so sweet!

Wasn't it glorious
she'd won first prize?

Elizabeth smiled
with cool gray eyes

and she wrapped her shawl
against the praise:

how soon there might come
more chilling days.

Turned to leave
without hesitating.

She was ready now,
and the world was waiting.

Eve Merriam

Harriet Tubman

Harriet Tubman didn't take no stuff
Wasn't scared of nothing neither
Didn't come into this world to be no slave
And wasn't going to stay one either

"Farewell!" she sang to her friends one night
She was mighty sad to leave 'em
But she ran away that dark, hot night
Ran looking for her freedom

She ran to the woods and she ran through the woods
With the slave catchers right behind her
And she kept on going till she got to the North
Where those mean men couldn't find her

Nineteen times she went back South
To get three hundred others
She ran for her freedom nineteen times
To save Black sisters and brothers
Harriet Tubman didn't take no stuff
Wasn't scared of nothing neither
Didn't come into this world to be no slave
And didn't stay one either

And didn't stay one either

Eloise Greenfield

Clara Barton

Brave Clara Barton
Stood beside her door,
And watched young soldiers
March away to war.

"The flags are very fine," she said,
"The drums and trumpets thrilling.
But what about the wounds
When the guns start killing?"

Clara Barton went to work
To help keep men alive,
And never got a moment's rest
Till eighteen sixty-five.

She washed and she bandaged,
She shooed away the flies,
She hurried in nurses,
She begged for supplies.

She cared for the wounded
And comforted the dying,
With no time for sleep
And still less for crying.

Clara Barton went abroad
When the war was ended.
Hoping for a little peace
Now that things had mended.

Clara found, as soon,
As her foot touched shore,
That she'd come just in time
For the Franco-Prussian War.

After that, her life, for her,
Held but little rest,
With famine in the East
And earthquakes in the West.

Floods, drowning Johnstown,
Hurricanes in Texas,
Fires, out in Michigan,
Things that fright and vex us.

In between the hurry calls,
Never at a loss,
She founded and established
The merciful Red Cross.

Battle, murder, sudden death,
Called for Clara Barton.
No one ever called in vain.
Clara was a Spartan.

Rosemary Benét

Ain't I a Woman?

That man over there say
    a woman needs to be helped into carriages
and lifted over ditches
    and to have the best place everywhere.
Nobody ever helped me into carriages
    or over mud puddles
        or gives me a best place...

    And ain't I a woman?
        Look at me
    Look at my arm!
        I have plowed and planted
    and gathered into barns
        and no man could head me...
    And ain't I a woman?
        I could work as much
    and eat as much as a man—
        when I could get to it—
    and bear the lash as well
        and ain't I a woman?

I have born 13 children
  and seen most all sold into slavery
and when I cried out a mother's grief
  none but Jesus heard me...
and ain't I a woman?
  that little man in black there say
a woman can't have as many rights as a man
  cause Christ wasn't born a woman
Where did your Christ come from?
  From God and a woman!
Man had nothing to do with him!
  If the first woman God ever made
was strong enough to turn the world
  upside down, all alone
together women ought to be able to turn it
  rightside up again.

Sojourner Truth
(adapted to poetry by Erlene Stetson)

Jeanne d'Arc

To be chosen—

my small body rejoices
at the words,
encases itself in silver
more lovely than silk.

Not to stay in the village
and marry the miller,
his babies heavy in my arms
as loaves of bread—

not to be God's bride
dressed in the long black robe
I've secretly named a shroud,
needing always to chasten myself
for my shimmering dreams—

but Christ's innocent mistress,
Lily of war!

Still, I can scarcely believe
how each time I speak
the sky brightens.

When the voice first came
from behind the dark trees
I sat for a long time, trembling.
Now my skin
burns, imagining how it will be,
the horse between my thighs,
a thousand men behind me
singing.

Susan Ludvigson

A Song of Greatness

When I hear the old men
Telling of heroes,
Telling of great deeds
Of ancient days,
When I hear that telling
Then I think within me
I too am one of these.

When I hear the people
Praising great ones,
Then I know that I too
Shall be esteemed,
I too when my time comes
Shall do mightily.

Mary Austin

Love Letter

Dear Samson,
I put your hair
in a jar
by the pear tree
near the well.
I been thinkin'
over what I done
and I still don't think
God gave you
all that strength
for you to kill
my people.

Love — Delilah

Carole E. Gregory

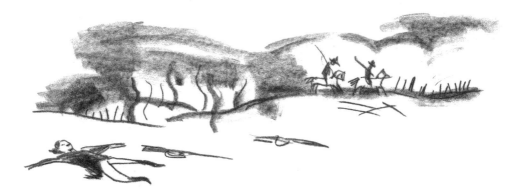

Captain Molly

On the bloody field of Monmouth
    Flashed the guns of Greene and Wayne,
Fiercely roared the tide of battle,
    Thick the sward was heaped with slain.
Foremost, facing death and danger,
    Hessian, horse, and grenadier,
In the vanguard, fiercely fighting,
    Stood an Irish Cannonier.

Loudly roared his iron cannon,
    Mingling ever in the strife,
And beside him, firm and daring,
    Stood his faithful Irish wife.
Of her bold contempt of danger
    Greene and Lee's brigades could tell,
Everyone knew "Captain Molly,"
    And the army loved her well.

Surged the roar of battle round them,
　　Swiftly flew the iron hail,
Forward dashed a thousand bayonets,
　　That lone battery to assail.
From the foeman's foremost columns
　　Swept a furious fusillade,
Mowing down the massed battalions
　　In the ranks of Greene's Brigade.

Fast and faster worked the gunner,
　　Soiled with powder, blood, and dust,
English bayonets shone before him,
　　Shot and shell around him burst;
Still he fought with reckless daring,
　　Stood and manned her long and well,
Till at last the gallant fellow
　　Dead—beside his cannon fell.

With a bitter cry of sorrow,
    And a dark and angry frown,
Looked that band of gallant patriots,
    At their gunner stricken down.
"Fall back, comrades, it is folly
    Thus to strive against the foe."
"No! not so," cried Irish Molly;
    "We can strike another blow."

Quickly leaped she to the cannon,
    In her fallen husband's place,
Sponged and rammed it fast and steady,
    Fired it in the foeman's face.
Flashed another ringing volley,
    Roared another from the gun;
"Boys, hurrah!" cried gallant Molly,
    "For the flag of Washington."

Fast they fly, these boasting Britons,
    Who in all their glory came,
With their brutal Hessian hirelings
    To wipe out our country's name.
Proudly floats the starry banner,
    Monmouth's glorious field is won.
And in triumph Irish Molly
    Stands beside her smoking gun.

William Collins

Notes

Page 15: "The Artist, Georgia O'Keeffe"—Georgia O'Keeffe (1887–1986) was an American painter famous for her New Mexican desert scenes and her beautiful semiabstract paintings of plants. She died in her late nineties after a long life of creativity.

Page 16: "[The Poet Emily]"—Emily Dickinson (1830–1886) was a great American poet, born and raised in Amherst, Massachusetts, who left us almost two thousand highly original poems, only several of which were published in her lifetime.

Page 17: "Sylvia Earle: Deep Ocean Explorer"—Sylvia Earle, born in Gibbstown, New Jersey, and the mother of two, is a research biologist and oceanographer. She is the author of *Exploring the Deep Frontier* and other books and has received many awards for her work in conservation and ocean study.

Page 19: "Girl with Sampler"—In the 1700s and 1800s, schoolgirls embroidered mottoes and sayings on square pieces of cloth to learn stitching or to show their skill. These strips of cloth were also covered with sample needlework patterns, and thus were known as samplers.

Page 22: "Conquering the Enemy"—Queen Boadicea, who died in A.D. 60, was the ruler of a tribe of Britons. Known as the Warrior Queen, she led a revolt against the Romans but was eventually defeated in battle.

Page 33: "Fastest Woman in the World"—In the 1988 Olympics, Florence Griffith Joyner won three gold medals: for the 100-meter, 200-meter, and

400-meter relays. She also won a silver for the 1600-meter relay. She died suddenly of a seizure at age thirty-seven in September 1998.

Page 36: "Aurelia Dobre: World Champion Gymnast"—At age fifteen, in 1987, Aurelia Dobre won the World All-Around Gymnastic Championship. She was the first and only Romanian girl to do so.

Page 37: "Wilma Rudolph"—As a child, Wilma Rudolph (1940–1994) wore a steel brace because of a crooked leg. She overcame this handicap to become, in 1960, the first American woman ever to win three gold medals in track and field competition. Five intertwined rings are a symbol of the Olympic games.

Page 38: "Joan Benoit"—Joan Benoit still holds the Olympic record for the women's marathon: 2 hours, 24 minutes, 52 seconds.

Page 39: "The Hamill Camel"—Dorothy Hamill won the gold medal for women's figure skating in the 1976 winter Olympics. The camel is a spin in which the skater balances on one leg and extends the other leg back.

Page 40: "First Lady of Sports"—Mildred "Babe" Didrikson Zaharias was an amazing all-around athlete. She broke three track and field world records in the 1932 Olympics and excelled in basketball, baseball, and tennis, and in later life became a professional golf champion.

Page 42: "WNBA Stars"—The Houston Comets have been the number-one team in the Women's National Basketball Association for 1997, 1998, and 1999. Cynthia Cooper and Sheryl Swoopes are two of their outstanding players. Both women have won gold medals on U.S. Olympic teams, Cooper in 1998 and Swoopes in 1996.

Page 50: "Brave New Heights"—In 1932, Amelia Earhart, age thirty-four, was the first woman to fly solo across the Atlantic Ocean. Five years later, on an attempted flight around the world, she disappeared somewhere over the Pacific Ocean. No trace of her, her navigator, or her plane was ever found.

Page 51: "Where Are You?"—Anne Frank was thirteen years old when she began her moving diary; she and her family hid from the Nazis in an Amsterdam warehouse for two years. Life-loving, she captures brilliantly a teenager's insecurities, hopes, joys, and irritations. She died at the

Bergen-Belsen concentration camp three months short of her sixteenth birthday and shortly before the Allied Forces arrived.

Page 52–53: "Fannie Lou Hamer"—A sharecropper in Mississippi, Fannie Lou Hamer (1917–1977) tried to register to vote in 1962 but was refused. The following year she succeeded, and she continued to work for voting rights. Later she was jailed and beaten for her activism. Her televised account of her experiences did much to help the civil rights movement.

Page 54–55: "The Many and the Few"—Rosa Parks's refusal to give up her seat in the front of a bus in Montgomery, Alabama, for a white person triggered the boycott of that bus system and helped bring about the civil rights movement in this country.

Page 56–58: "from Elizabeth Blackwell"—Elizabeth Blackwell (1821–1910) was the first woman doctor of medicine in modern times.

Page 59: "Harriet Tubman"—Born a slave in 1821, Harriet Tubman escaped to the North in 1849, and in the 1850s returned to the South nineteen times to lead many hundreds of slaves to freedom. She was the most famous leader of the Underground Railroad. During the Civil War she was a nurse, scout, and spy for the Union Army.

Page 60–61: "Clara Barton"—Born in Oxford, Massachusetts, Clara Barton (1821–1912) was a teacher in early life and established various free schools in New Jersey. She went into hospital service when the Civil War began and carried out at her own expense a systematic search for missing soldiers. She is best known as the founder of the American Red Cross in 1881 and for her dedicated relief work in many disasters thereafter.

Page 62–63: "Ain't I a Woman?"—Sojourner Truth (1797–1883) was the name taken by Isabella Baumfree when she began to travel and preach against slavery in the 1840s, the first black woman to do so. With her commanding voice, her famous wit, and her faith in God, she became one of the best known American abolitionists. This poem was adapted by Erlene Stetson from a speech given at the Women's Rights Convention in Akron, Ohio, in 1852.

Page 64–65: "Jeanne d'Arc"—During the British siege of Orleans, France, in the fifteenth century, Jeanne d'Arc (or Joan of Arc), a simple peasant girl inspired by heavenly voices, led a small army and forced the British to withdraw. She won other battles, always in male attire, and was eventually captured by the British, tried as a witch by a French church tribunal, and burned at the stake in 1431. She was officially declared innocent in 1456 and canonized as a saint in 1920.

Page 67: "Love Letter"—In the Bible story, Delilah, a Philistine woman, was the mistress of Samson, a man of enormous strength and an enemy of the Philistines. Learning that Samson's strength lay in his hair, she cut it off while he was asleep, and the Philistines were able to capture him. She has always been thought of as a betrayer. The poet here thinks differently.

Page 68–71: "Captain Molly"—Mary McCauley was known as Molly Pitcher because she carried water to the wounded soldiers during the battle of Monmouth in the Revolutionary War. When her husband, a cannoneer, was felled at his post, she manned his cannon throughout the rest of the battle. George Washington made her an officer for her bravery.

Acknowledgments

Thanks first to Marjorie Mir, Nina Pratt, Susan Sermoneta, Rosamund Thalmann, and my agent, Marian Reiner, all good friends who helped in one way or another in the making of this book.

Every effort has been made to trace the ownership of all copyrighted material and to secure the necessary permissions to reprint these selections. In the event of any question arising as to the use of any material, the editor and the publisher, while expressing regret for any inadvertent error, will be happy to make the necessary correction in future printings.

Grateful acknowledgment is made for permission to print the following poems:

"the drum" by Nikki Giovanni. From *Spin a Soft Black Song* by Nikki Giovanni. Copyright © 1971, 1985 by Nikki Giovanni. Reprinted by permission of Farrar, Straus, and Giroux, LLC.

"Yes, It Was My Grandmother" by Luci Tapahonso. From *A Breeze Swept Through* by Luci Tapahonso. Copyright © 1987 by Luci Tapahonso. Reprinted by permission of West End Press.

"Pioneer Girl Driving West" by Ann Turner. Published as "Driving" in *Mississippi Mud*. Text copyright © 1997 by Ann Turner. Reprinted by permission of HarperCollins Publishers.

"The Rebel" by Mari Evans. From *I Am a Black Woman*, published by William Morrow & Co., 1970. Reprinted by permission of the author.

"from 'Adventures of Isabel'" by Ogden Nash. First stanza of "Adventures